MW01491042

ABC's of Oregon

By Andy Bauer

To Sahmie

My heart and soul. Without your love, ideas, edits, and encouragement this book never would have been. Here's to more awesome adventures in this amazing state of ours.

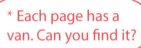

* Each page has a van. Can you find it?

Copyright 2024 by Andy Bauer
All rights reserved.

ISBN: 979-8-9918621-1-0
2nd Edition
Puddle Foot Publishing

A

Astoria

Where the mighty Columbia meets the Pacific
There is a town that's just terrific.
Where giant ships cross a dangerous bar
To deliver their cargo to ports near and far.

B Bend

Walk by the Deschutes or go for a float
Ski on Mt. Bachelor but bring a warm coat.
You can see the Three Sisters and Broken Top too
If you ascend Pilot Butte for the ultimate view.

C

Crater Lake

Mt. Mazama erupted leaving a caldera behind
Filled with water so blue it will boggle your mind.
Take a trip by boat to the Phantom Ship
Hike on Wizard Island or take a cold dip.

Depoe Bay

This tiny harbor has so much to share
Go see grey whales splash their tails in the air.
When big storms roll in, watch the spouting horn spray
A poncho's a must when you're at Depoe Bay.

E Eugene

Known to sports fans as Tracktown USA
It's the birthplace of Nike back in the day.
It's a university city with so much to do
Join a frisbee game and a drum circle too.

* Tickets to Autzen might cost a few bucks
  But you won't mind a bit when you're screaming, Go Ducks!

F

Fossil

Fossilized horses and saber-toothed cat
For mammalian paleontology, this is where it's at.
If digging up fossils isn't for you
Go check out the rodeo, buckaroo.

G Columbia River Gorge

The Columbia River created this wonder
Where backpackers sweat and waterfalls thunder.
Multnomah Falls and Wahkeena too
The trails are calling there's hiking to do!

Hood River

The Hood River's mouth is an incredible space
With windsurfers and kiteboarders all over the place.
Head up the valley for orchards and fruit
You'll get views of Wy'east and Pahto to boot.

Imnaha

This eastern Oregon area is rugged and unique
High grasslands and mountain valleys, it isn't for the weak.
The Nez Perce wintered here, their horses they would bring
And with the warmer weather, they would leave in the spring.

J

John Day Fossil Beds National Monument

A national monument by the name of John Day
Has a Painted Hills Unit that's out of the way.
The color of these hills just can't be beat
Thanks to the geology right under your feet.

K

Klamath Falls

Stroll the shore of the largest lake in the state
The pelican viewing is really first rate.
Hike the hills above town near the giant K
The views of Mt. Shasta will brighten your day.

La Grande

Today you'll pass trucks on I-84
But during the Oregon Trail, there were wagons galore.
They crossed the Blue Mountains just west of La Grande
At the interpretive site their ruts still mark the land.

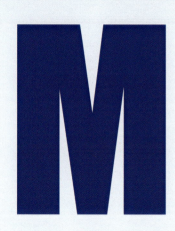

Malheur Lake

Just southeast of Burns and north of the Steens
Lies a place that's the stuff of all birder's dreams.
Birds fly to these wetlands in flocks to partake
And pause their migration at Malheur Lake.

Newport

Newport sits astride lovely Yaquina Bay
Where the tide ebbs and flows two times in a day.
Here fishing boats sail to catch seafood dinner
The chowder is great and the aquarium's a winner.

O

Owyhee River

This desert river was named Owyhee
For three lost fur trappers from Hawaii.
With 1,000 foot cliffs and rapids galore
This river keeps rafters begging for more.

P

Portland

The City of Roses is a city with spark
From high Council Crest to Waterfront Park.
Where the mighty Columbia and Willamette meet
Portland chooses to dance to its own unique beat.

Q Quartz Mountain Sno-park

Between Lakeview and Bly
this place might catch your eye
pull over and give snowmobiling a try.

For a small sno-park fee
You can cross country ski
And zoom across white frosty snow, yippee!

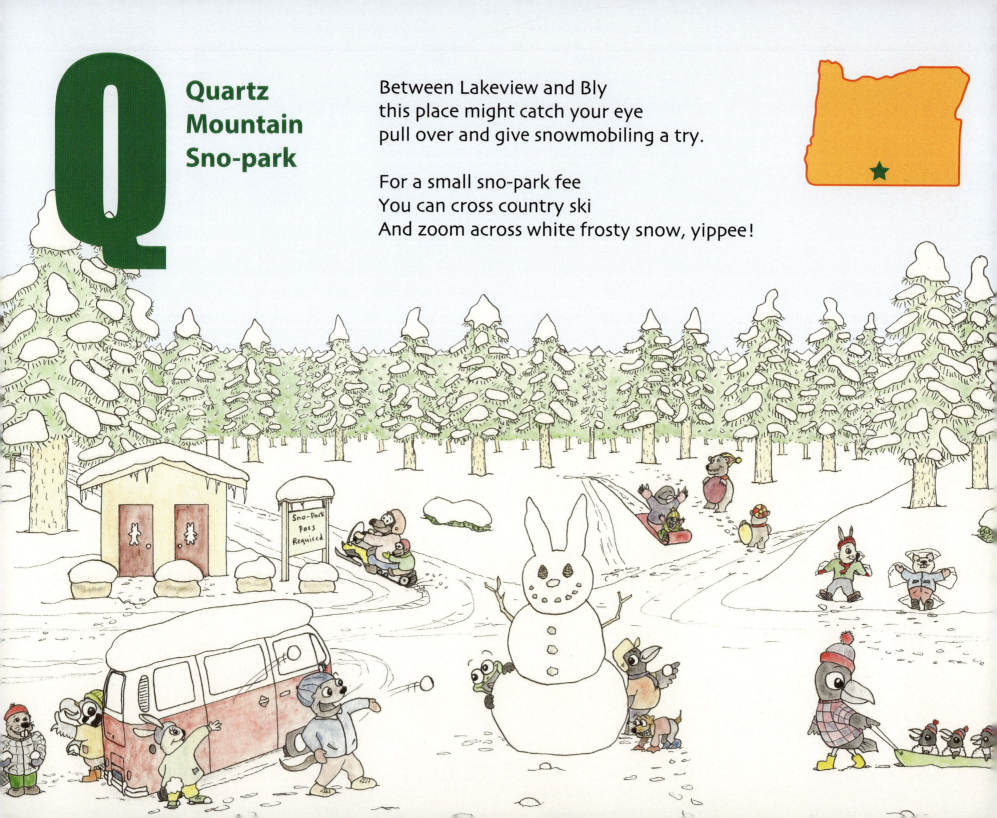

R

Rogue River

Ride the zooming jet boats to thrill and excite
Or raft the raging river and camp for the night.
The Rogue has its secrets as the backpackers know
Bring a love of the wild and a map if you go.

S

Salem

Salem's the capital of the 33rd state
Where its elected officials meet to legislate.
Follow the Mill Race to the Willamette's shore
There's a riverfront carousel and island to explore.

T

Trout Creek

It starts in the mountains and runs through sagebrush
In the summer it's a trickle but during storms it's a rush.
It flows to Alvord Lake below the mighty Steens
Where its waters evaporate leaving salty sheens.

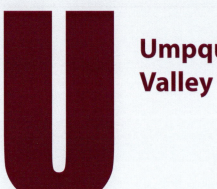

Umpqua Valley

In this golden valley follow the Umpqua River's flow
Passing scenic vineyards and farmland as you go.
Fishing, rafting, camping, and more
Who knows what adventures you'll find by its shore.

V

Veneta

Outside Veneta in July every year
Thousands gather in good health and good cheer.
They come in wild costumes with plenty of flair
To frolic outside at the Oregon Country Fair.

W

Wallowa Mountains

Just south of Joseph and Enterprise
These mountains reach up and touch the skies.
Backpackers sweat as they climb Eagle Cap
Then find a nice campsite lakeside for a nap.

X

Captain Xenolith

Climbing Smith Rock's volcanic tuff
Experienced climbers just can't get enough.
Over 1,000 routes with fun names can be done
Captain Xenolith is an example of one.

Yachats

Yachats in the summer is the place to be
So quaintly perched on the shore by the sea.
But its rocky cliffs may be at their most fun
Once winter's big storms and their waves have begun.

Z

Zigzag

Many pass Zigzag on their way to Mt. Hood
Where the hiking is swell and the skiing is good.
But at the end of the day they'll pull over their ride
And gather with friends by the cozy fireside.

Glossary

Alvord Lake A seasonal lake east of Steens Mountain that collects water from streams like Trout Creek and dries up in the summer.

Autzen (AWt-zen) Autzen stadium is the football stadium for the University of Oregon Ducks.

Bar An area of shallow sand or gravel in a river which can be dangerous for ships to cross.

Blue Mountains A mountain range in Northeastern Oregon made of some of the oldest rocks in the state.

Broken Top A highly eroded volcano next to the Three Sisters.

Buckaroo A cowboy.

Caldera (call-DARE-a) A large sunken crater-like hole left behind by some volcanic eruptions.

Columbia The Columbia River is the largest river on the west coast of the United States.

Council Crest A hilltop park high atop the West Hills of Portland.

Deschutes (Da-SHOOT-s) A beautiful river in Central Oregon that runs through Bend from the Cascade Mountains to the Columbia River.

Eagle Cap A high central peak in the Wallowa Mountains.

Gorge A deep valley with steep walled sides.

Grey Whales The most common whales off the Oregon Coast.

Mammalian Paleontology
(mam-A-lee-an pail-E-on-tol-oh-jee)
The study of ancient mammals and their fossils.

Mill Race The Mill Race is a manmade creek that runs through Salem from Mill Creek to the Willamette River.

Mt. Bachelor An extinct volcano near Bend, that has a ski area on top.

Mt. Mazama The name given to the volcano that erupted and created Crater Lake.

Mt. Shasta A large Cascade Range volcano in northern California.

Mt. Hood The tallest mountain in Oregon. Also known by its Native American name, Wy'east.

Multnomah Falls The tallest waterfall in the state and a major tourist attraction in the Columbia River Gorge.

Nez Perce (nez purse) The Nez Perce Tribe is a Native American tribe who have resided since time immemorial on the high plateau in parts of Oregon, Washington, Idaho, and Montana.

Oregon Trail A two thousand mile wagon route used by settlers to access land in Oregon between the 1840's and the 1860's.

Pahto/Klickitat (PAW-too / CLICK-eh-tat) Two Native American names for the second tallest mountain in Washington. Also known as Mt. Adams.

Phantom Ship A small rocky island in Crater Lake that looks like a ship.

Pilot Butte A small cinder cone volcano in the city of Bend with a drive up view.

Smith Rock Refers to Smith Rock State Park. A park with stunning cliff walls along the Crooked River that is a popular rock climbing destination.

Spouting Horn A hole in a rocky shoreline that sprays water when waves crash into it.

Steens Refers to Steens Mountain in southeastern Oregon.

Three Sisters Three Cascade volcanos that are near each other, North, Middle and South Sister.

Tuff A type of rock created when the hot volcanic ash of an eruption falls to the ground and welds itself together.

Wahkeena Falls A beautiful cascading waterfall close to Multnomah Falls in the Columbia River Gorge.

Waterfront Park A park along the Willamette River in downtown Portland where festivals happen and large ships can dock.

Willamette (WILL-am-et) The Willamette River is a major river that drains the Willamette Valley which includes many large cities such as Eugene, Corvallis, Salem, and Portland.

Wizard Island A cinder cone volcano that is an island inside Crater Lake.

Wy'east (WHY-east) The tallest mountain in Oregon. Also known as Mt. Hood.

Xenolith (zeen-O-lith) A rock trapped within another rock. Xenoliths in the volcanic rock found at Smith Rock State Park help rock climbers climb.

Yaquina Bay (YA-quin-a BAY) Where the Yaquina River meets the ocean in the city of Newport.

* Like many location names in Oregon, the name Yaquina is derived from the name of the first people to live there, the Yaquina Tribe.

My Oregon Travel Journal

There are so many amazing Oregon places to experience. Can you visit all 26 places in this book? When you go to a location, take the time to write down some details to help you remember your special visit. When did you go? Who did you go with? What was a special memory you made? Don't forget to bring this book along too. You can take a picture of yourself with the book and send it to ABC's of Oregon on Instagram and we'll post your picture to inspire others to get out there and fall in love with Oregon too. Happy adventures!

Astoria

Date: _____

Travel Buddies:

_____

Highlights: _____

_____

_____

Bend

Date: _____

Travel Buddies:

_____

Highlights: _____

_____

_____

Crater Lake

Date: _____

Travel Buddies:

_____

Highlights: _____

_____

_____

Depoe Bay

Date: _____

Travel Buddies:

_____

Highlights: _____

_____

_____

Eugene

Date: _____

Travel Buddies:

_____

Highlights: _____

_____

_____

Fossil

Date: _____

Travel Buddies:

_____

Highlights: _____

_____

_____

Columbia River Gorge

Date: _____

Travel Buddies:

_____

Highlights: _____

_____

_____

Hood River

Date: _____

Travel Buddies:

_____

Highlights: _____

_____

_____

Imnaha

Date: _____

Travel Buddies:

_____

Highlights: _____

_____

_____

John Day Fossil Beds

Date: _____

Travel Buddies:

_____

Highlights: _____

_____

_____

Klamath Falls

Date: _____

Travel Buddies:

_____

Highlights: _____

_____

_____

La Grande

Date: _____

Travel Buddies:

_____

Highlights: _____

_____

_____

Malheur Lake

Date: _____

Travel Buddies:

_____

Highlights: _____

_____

_____

Newport

Date: _____

Travel Buddies:

_____

Highlights: _____

_____

_____

Owyhee River

Date: _____

Travel Buddies:

_____

Highlights: _____

_____

_____

Portland

Date: _____

Travel Buddies:

_____

Highlights: _____

_____

_____

Quartz Mountain Sno-park

Date: _____

Travel Buddies:

_____

Highlights: _____

_____

_____

Rogue River

Date: _____

Travel Buddies: _____

Highlights: _____

_____

_____

Salem

Date: _____

Travel Buddies:

_____

Highlights: _____

_____

_____

Trout Creek
(Alvord Lake/Steens Mountain Area)

Date: _____

Travel Buddies:

_____

Highlights: _____

_____

_____

Umpqua Valley

Date: _____

Travel Buddies:

_____

Highlights: _____

_____

_____

Veneta

Date: _____

Travel Buddies:

_____

Highlights: _____

_____

_____

Wallowa Mountains

Date: _____

Travel Buddies:

_____

Highlights: _____

_____

_____

Captain Xenolith
(Smith Rock State Park)

Date: _____

Travel Buddies:

_____

Highlights: _____

_____

_____

Yachats

Date: _____

Travel Buddies:

_____

Highlights: _____

_____

_____

Zigzag

Date: _____

Travel Buddies:

_____

Highlights: _____

_____

_____

Oregon

Astoria

Columbia
River Gorge
Hood River

Imnaha

Portland

Zigzag

La Grande

Fossil

Depoe Bay

Salem

Wallowa
Mountains

Newport

John Day Fossil Beds
National Monument
Painted Hills Unit

Yachats

Captain Xenolith
(Smith Rock State Park)

Veneta   Eugene

Bend

Umpqua Valley

Malheur Lake National
Wildlife Refuge

Crater Lake
National Park

Owyhee River

Rogue River

Quartz Mountain
Sno-park

Klamath Falls

Trout Creek